Series / Number 02-013

Arms Races, Diplomacy, and Recurring Behavior: Lessons from Two Cases

BARRY H. STEINER
California State University, Long Beach

SAGE PUBLICATIONS / Beverly Hills / London

Copyright © 1973 by Sage Publications, Inc.

Printed in the United States of America

All rights reserved. No part of this book may be reproduced
or utilized in any form or by any means, electronic or mechanical,
including photocopying, recording, or by any
information storage and retrieval system, without permission in writing
from the publisher.

For information address:

SAGE PUBLICATIONS, INC.
275 South Beverly Drive
Beverly Hills, California 90212

SAGE PUBLICATIONS, INC.
St George's House / 44 Hatton Garden
London EC1N 8ER

International Standard Book Number 0-8039-0222-0

Library of Congress Catalog Card No. L.C. 73-76399

FIRST PRINTING

When citing a professional paper, please use the proper form. Remember to cite the correct Sage Professional Paper series title and include the paper number. One of the two following formats can be adapted (depending on the style manual used):

(1) CAPORASO, J. A. (1972) Functionalism and Regional Integration: A Logical and Empirical Assessment. Sage Professional Paper in International Studies 02-004. Beverly Hills and London: Sage Pubns.

OR

(2) Caporaso, James A., *Functionalism and Regional Integration: A Logical and Empirical Assessment.* Beverly Hills and London: Sage Professional Paper in International Studies 02-004, 1972.

CONTENTS

Introduction 5
Weapons Procurement and Technological Change 7
Weapons Procurement and Diplomatic Crisis 8
Weapons Procurement and Détente 16
An Argument for Relevance 18
On Explaining Recurring Arms Race Behavior 21
Epilogue 27
Notes 35
References 39

Arms Races, Diplomacy, and Recurring Behavior: Lessons from Two Cases

BARRY H. STEINER
California State University, Long Beach

INTRODUCTION

An arms race exists when two nations, or two sets of nations, each reserving to themselves the right and strength to make war, enter into repeated, competitive, and reciprocal adjustments of their war-making capacities. It is a disturbing condition, and a recurring one.[1]

One major shortcoming of the growing arms race literature is the lack of any systematic attempt to show how variations in the perceived likelihood of war, induced mainly by factors outside the ongoing competition, affect the pace of competitive arms procurement. This article is intended to remedy that shortcoming. It attempts to show how two historical instances of battleship accumulation—the first between England, France, and Russia roughly between the years 1884 and 1905, and the second between England and Germany from 1898 to 1914—adjusted to changes in the perceived likelihood of war and in perceived weapons efficiency.

That an arms race adjusts to variations in military capability is clear; that it can also adjust to variations in hostile intent is less apparent. It might plausibly be expected that increased tension would lead to an acceleration of the competition, and that improved relations, or détente, would lead to a slowdown in the race. But neither of these hypotheses has ever been confirmed.

AUTHOR'S NOTE: *The author wishes to thank Warner R. Schilling, Louis Henkin, and Arno Mayer for helpful comments and criticism.*

The major finding of the present study is that procurement is only imperfectly related to changes in the way policymakers perceive the international diplomatic climate. Perceptions of an increased likelihood of war bring about an acceleration of procurement, but a marked reduction in the perceived likelihood of war does not bring about any slackening in the pace of procurement. Factors that affect the form of arms competition, such as technological change, do not work against this effect. Efforts should be made to apply these findings to the superpower competition presently under way and to explain the apparent inconsistency in the findings.

The role of technological change in arms races has often been remarked upon but insufficiently analysed. One authority (Huntington, 1958: 54, 71-76) distinguishes two types of armaments competition: quantitative, where the race centers around the numbers of weapons available to or desired by the racers; and qualitative, where the race centers around the production of more efficient, as opposed to more numerous weapons. However, the competitions to be examined in this article contain elements of numerical *and* technological rivalry. They were most importantly quantitative in character (Huntington, 1958: 71ff.), but there was also an element of technological competition in them. Arthur J. Marder (1940: 8), a leading historian of the British navy, refers to the "bewilderingly rapid progress in naval construction [whose] far-reaching consequences . . . lay at the root of much of the naval expansion after 1880." Yet it is not clear why technical progress, hastening as it did the obsolescence of weapons previously procured, should not instead have depressed the accumulation of weaponry.

It is argued here that insights derived from the two competitions examined can and should be applied to other competitions occurring in other periods. States have always disagreed among themselves on issues they regard as vital, and this disagreement has often been paralleled by a propensity to compete in the accumulation and improvement of armaments.[2] But states may disagree more or less at different times, the design of weapons may change substantially or not at all, and the pace of the quantitative armaments race may vary accordingly. An attempt will be made here to discover regularities amidst these changes.

Any analysis of the problem of arms races must attempt to shed some light on the present-day Soviet-American competition, which, though under way for a quarter of a century, remains poorly understood. The analysis must be especially prepared to assist in the understanding of what seems a paradox: the Cold War, by most accounts, has eased in recent years into détente, while the Soviet-American arms race has gone forward in seemingly unabated fashion (Wiesner, 1967: 6). It has been observed that after 1957, American weapons procurement, far from proceeding on the assumption that Soviet-American war was likely, has been based on the fear of an irrationally motivated or accidental attack on the United States by the Soviet Union (Wiesner, 1967: 464). A new rationale was found by American policy planners for pushing the arms race ahead, even though Soviet-American hostility diminished.

Absence of enough reliable, published data about the Soviet-American competition precludes direct analysis of that competition; but a great deal of comparable information is available for the period 1884-1914, particularly about the diplomatic and shipbuilding policies of Great Britain, the leading naval power of the era.[3] British shipbuilding and diplomacy will be the focal points of this article; sufficient changes occurred in the perceived likelihood of war, the perceived technical efficiency of weaponry, and in the pace of the arms race to yield numerous examples of how procurement adjusted to changes in the political climate and to changes in the design of strategic weaponry, as British policymakers saw them.[4] These examples will be collected with a view to providing convincing evidence for propositions about how, why, and to what degree arms races are affected by perceptions of policymakers about changes in technology and in the likelihood of war. The propositions, in turn, can then be applied to the Soviet-American competition of the present day.

WEAPONS PROCUREMENT AND TECHNOLOGICAL CHANGE

The impact of perceived technological changes on the accumulation of battleships may be most conveniently discussed first. Such changes helped alternately to depress and to accelerate battleship building, but they were overshadowed in their impact on naval procurement by more potent causal factors.

For most of the time period from 1884 to 1914, British naval leaders saw no challenge to the usefulness of battleships in a future naval war, and therefore they saw no reason not to build more of such ships. But technological change, by its impact on shipbuilding design, did on occasion serve to depress the pace of British naval construction. In the years 1885-1888, for example, the British—along with the French—lost confidence in the viability of their ironclads in the face of the threat posed by the torpedo. During 1886, 1887, and 1888, the British and French failed to start a single new battleship. Another instance when the British

Admiralty lost confidence in the viability of its ironclads occurred in 1904, the year the Admiralty decided upon rapid construction of the all-big-gun *Dreadnought* battleship. Here again the threat posed by the torpedo to the battleship led British naval officials to reduce their estimates of the efficiency of the battleship in naval war and to limit the number of ironclads built.

Sometimes, however, technological change militated in favor of expanding the quantitative arms race. This happened in 1889, when the large battleship provisions of the British Naval Defense Act were facilitated by advances in armor plate, improving the protection of the ironclad against the torpedo. Technological change also contributed to acceleration of the arms race when in 1892 the British Admiralty designed an improved torpedo boat, or destroyer, which again enhanced the defense of the battleship in the face of torpedo boat construction by other naval powers. The Spencer program (named after the First Lord of the Admiralty), drafted in 1893 and launched in 1894, allowed for the construction of numerous additional battleships.

Generalizations about the impact of technological changes on the race are not easy to make. The British Admiralty wanted new, expensive ships, but it did not have a research and technology budget large enough to ascertain the viability of the latest shipbuilding designs. Moreover, though shipbuilding by naval rivals sometimes acutely threatened the potential survivability of British vessels in a naval engagement, the British Admiralty was never prepared to reject its battleship fleet as the primary vehicle for maintaining control of the seas. Consequently, the government on occasion (1885, 1889) was to sanction the building of vessels that were shortly afterward demonstrated by Admiralty calculations to be exceedingly vulnerable to attack (especially from the torpedo, but also from opposing battleships). But if the Admiralty was to take what proved later from a technical viewpoint to be serious risks in constructing certain classes of vessels, this would indicate that in periods of rapid technological change, naval officials (as well as civilian members of the government) were sensitive to factors other than technology in deciding to accelerate shipbuilding. Particularly important among these other factors was the series of diplomatic crises between England and other major powers.[5]

WEAPONS PROCUREMENT AND DIPLOMATIC CRISIS

How does the accumulation of armaments adjust to changes in the perceived likelihood of war? There are a number of occasions in the period

1884-1914 where acceleration in shipbuilding does appear to be accounted for, at least in part, by the coming of a diplomatic crisis. These occasions are frequent and impressive enough to suggest a strong causal relationship between an increase in the perceived likelihood of war and accelerated shipbuilding. They will be briefly outlined.

(1) In December 1884, popular clamor about the state of the navy led to a parliamentary debate and the spelling out by the First Lord of the Admiralty of a projected program of shipbuilding, including four ironclads, five belted cruisers, two torpedo rams, ten scouts and thirty torpedo boats, for the following year. Admiralty spokesmen in Parliament indicated that a portion of these vessels would be financed by a supplementary appropriation, but the government had not yet decided what that appropriation would include. The First Lord wanted to use it mainly to protect British commerce—for example, by fortifying harbors; naval leaders were most interested in acquiring more sea-going torpedo vessels to protect existing ironclads, though they demanded that new ironclads be included in the supplemental as well.

Prime Minister William Gladstone was opposed to supplemental expenditure on ironclads and succeeded in deadlocking the Cabinet when it considered the supplemental program first in December 1884 and then in March 1885. But in the latter month an Anglo-Russian diplomatic confrontation came about when a Russian force attacked an Afghan army that the British government was resolved to protect. On April 26, with the crisis persisting, the First Lord submitted the naval estimates for 1885 to Parliament. Of the four battleships which had been projected by the First Lord in December, two were included in the 1885 estimates and—it was later revealed—the two others were begun in 1885 but not financed until the following year. On April 28, the government sought parliamentary approval for a large vote of credit to prepare for war with Russia; included within the vote of credit was an allocation to finance the building of forty torpedo boats that were intended to serve as destroyers defending British armorclads against Russian torpedo boat attacks during anticipated naval operations in the Baltic. The building of the torpedo boats was a response to a recent decision by the Russian government to build an equal number of such vessels.

(2) For three years after British approval of the 1885 program, no further large shipbuilding programs were projected by the Admiralty. But in 1888 another diplomatic issue helped engender new large-scale shipbuilding demands. Beginning in February 1888, and for some months

thereafter, the British government was involved in a Franco-Italian war scare, committed to the defense of Italy against what seemed an imminent French attack. The Admiralty became preoccupied during this crisis with the threat of French attacks against British commerce in the Far East, but only with difficulty could it spare ships from the Mediterranean to reinforce the Far Eastern fleet. Moreover, naval intelligence officials and the Prime Minister, Lord Salisbury, concluded from the crisis that Franco-Russian cooperation was a contingency in preparation for which British naval construction should be determined. Intelligence officials pointed to the possible implications of French loans being channeled for the first time to Russia; and Salisbury was being persuaded by German leaders (who only a year earlier had helped bring about two Mediterranean agreements in which Britain, Italy and Austria-Hungary pledged to act together in event of Russian provocations) that the threat posed to Italy in Western Europe was related to the threat posed by Russia to the Balkans and Turkey in the East. In July the government asked the Admiralty Board (composed of leading naval officials) to define confidentially the naval requirements for, among other possibilities, a war between England on one hand, and France and Russia on the other, in which the British were committed to the defense of Constantinople. The Board obliged and drafted a large shipbuilding program entailing the start of ten battleships in a three-year period—part of a larger program that became known as the Naval Defense Act—to remedy naval deficiencies.

(3) With shipbuilding under the Naval Defense Act under way, the Admiralty saw fit to take further steps in response to parallel activity in France and Russia, and approved in April 1892 a projected program highlighted by seven battleships; the First Lord approved the program in August 1892. However, a subsequent Admiralty decision to accelerate completion of Naval Defense Act construction before doing substantial work on additional ships and an unfortunate battleship collision brought postponements, so that by late 1893 only one of the seven projected battleships had been begun, though the government had approved the building of two others. In this lethargic state of naval affairs, an Anglo-French crisis took place in July 1893, when French gunboats forced their way up the Mekong River to Bangkok, the capital of neutral Siam, and subsequently blockaded the country. The Admiralty Board used the crisis to increase its shipbuilding demands: late in July it asked for two new battleships in 1894 and three in 1895; in August it asked for seven (a number equal to the size of the Russian Black Sea fleet) to be completed by 1898; late in the year it asked for ten completed new battleships by 1898.

The First Lord of the Admiralty and the Foreign Minister now found diplomatic and strategic justification for accelerated shipbuilding. Even before the Siam crisis had taken place, British diplomacy in the Mediterranean had been based upon a commitment to defend Constantinople against a combined attack by France and Russia, while the British government did not have a navy strong enough to make such a defense feasible. But the chances of such a bluff being exposed by foreign powers, in the opinion of the First Lord and the Foreign Minister, were greater in the wake of diplomatic crisis, and both thought it necessary to take compensating action accordingly. For the First Lord, Earl Spencer, the chances that the policy of bluff would be exposed made it necessary to strengthen British naval forces in the Mediterranean, where the British squadron was weaker than the French, by a large program of shipbuilding. For the Foreign Minister, on the other hand, fear that the bluff would be exposed militated in the direction of strengthening the bluff further. Some months after the Siam crisis, the Austrian Foreign Minister revealed to his British counterpart, Lord Rosebery, that in view of the unstable domestic conditions in Italy at that time, Austria would come to terms with Russia unless Britain reasserted her traditional commitments in the Mediterranean. For Austria, this meant in part an increase in the British navy. Rosebery, whose diplomacy required the assistance of the Triple Alliance in a war with Russia, seems to have looked upon such an increase as a prerequisite for any further active British diplomacy in the Mediterranean; it was for him the best way to reinstate Austrian confidence in the British diplomatic position, though it did not alter the fundamental weakness of that position. The program of seven battleships, comprising the first installment of the Spencer program, was approved by the Cabinet in April 1894 and commenced in fiscal 1894.

(4) According to an understanding reached before Cabinet approval of the Spencer program between the First Lord of the Admiralty and naval leaders, the First Lord would press the Cabinet to begin three additional British battleships if France or Russia should together begin more than the five battleships the British Admiralty anticipated in those countries for 1894. Late in 1895 the Admiralty cited this agreement in support of its request to build three battleships in the face of steady new Russian construction. Again also, there was trouble on the diplomatic front, this time over three distinct issues in different parts of the world which became acute in rapid succession. In the first of these, the British government concluded that a Russian invasion of Constantinople was imminent. The government, still committed publicly to the defense of Turkish sover-

eignty, debated sending a British fleet up through the Dardanelles Straits as a preventive measure, but decided not to do so because of the weakness of the British naval position. The Admiralty used this occasion also to increase its shipbuilding demands for fiscal 1896 from three to five battleships, ostensibly in response to the building of second-class as well as first-class French and Russian ironclads; the former, it maintained, were of first-class strength in home waters.

The Cabinet did not immediately accept the increased Admiralty demands, because of the resistance of the Chancellor of the Exchequer, Michael Hicks-Beach. But Hicks-Beach was to change his mind after two additional crises occurred during the budget-drafting period: one with the United States over a boundary dispute between Venezuela and British Guiana (December 1895), and the other with Germany over the Kruger telegram from the German Emperor following the abortive Jameson raid in South Africa (January 1896). The Chancellor of the Exchequer agreed to the Admiralty demands, specifically citing the changed international conditions as requiring them.[6]

(5) Again, in 1898, an upturn in diplomatic pressures on the British government coincided with increased shipbuilding pressures. In March 1898, the Chinese government leased Port Arthur as a naval base to Russia in the face of opposition from a British government committed to maintain the political status quo in China, triggering another Anglo-Russian confrontation. The British Cabinet chose ultimately to acquiesce in the Russian presence at Port Arthur, while demanding a comparable naval base nearby as a concession to Great Britain. Earlier the same month, the British government learned of a Russian decision to begin a large new shipbuilding program, and the new crisis with Russia focused the attention of the government on the implications of fulfillment of the new Russian program for the size of the Russian Far East fleet. In June 1898 the First Lord of the Admiralty came to the Cabinet to ask for a supplementary program of naval construction in response to the recently announced Russian program, citing information to the effect that the Russian fleet based at Port Arthur would ultimately consist of six to eight battleships as well as lighter craft. He cited two justifications for increased shipbuilding that had been agreed upon by the Cabinet previously: (a) the number of British battleships had to be equal to those of France and Russia at a minimum; and (b) if shipbuilding in any strong naval power materially disturbed the naval balance of forces, the British shipbuilding program would have to be reconsidered. But though the First Lord defended the supplementary program as "parallel action" (to keep pace with Russian

building commencing in 1898), the British built one more ship than was called for by his definition of minimum British requirements. Four new Russian battleships appeared definitely ordered in 1898, and the British had earlier matched one of them in provisions of the regular estimates for 1898 when that vessel was still in a projected state; yet four battleships were included in the supplementary British program.

(6) In January 1901, the First Lord of the Admiralty, Lord Selborne, came to the Cabinet with a request for a fixed shipbuilding program, shaped to achieve a predetermined standard of naval strength in relation to France and Russia. The Cabinet rejected the request at that time and did not reconsider it in deliberations on the naval budget for 1902, Selborne choosing not to introduce it when the Cabinet accepted without change his shipbuilding proposal for that year. The Admiralty's proposed program of new shipbuilding was considerably reduced in fiscal 1902 from what it had been in 1901. In April 1902, a diplomatic confrontation took place between England and Germany over conflicting claims in the Yangtze Valley, and Selborne took advantage of the crisis to gain support among Cabinet officials for his fixed shipbuilding program. He quickly consulted with the Foreign Minister and then with the Prime Minister, citing the increased need for a fixed shipbuilding policy in the light of German antagonism to England in the Far East. During Cabinet discussions on the naval budget for 1903, Selborne reintroduced his fixed shipbuilding program idea, entailing a program highlighted by three battleships and four armored cruisers over each of the next four years, citing in part as justification German hostility and the steady buildup of the German navy (then going on under terms of the second German navy law of 1900). The Cabinet accepted the fixed shipbuilding program in the autumn of 1902.

(7) German shipbuilding persisted in the first decade of the twentieth century, but the British naval position was aided by French naval stagnation and the decimation of the Russian navy in the Russo-Japanese War (1904-1905). In 1908 British capital shipbuilding consisted of one battleship and one battle cruiser; but in May 1908 the British Admiralty Board agreed to build a total of four, and if necessary, six battleships and battle cruisers in 1909, and this agreement had the support of the Foreign Minister, Edward Grey. Late in 1908 information available to the British government indicated, first, that projected German shipbuilding would bring Britain behind Germany in dreadnoughts in three years; and second, Germany was accelerating the building of dreadnoughts beyond the pace set in the schedule of the second German navy law (as amended with larger

appropriations in 1906). As Cabinet debate on the 1909 naval budget intensified, the Admiralty in January 1909 increased its demands to eight dreadnoughts (including all-big-gun battleships and battle cruisers); and the Cabinet agreed the following month to a compromise budget whereby four dreadnoughts would be laid down immediately, and four more later in the year if they were found necessary.

In this period, two diplomatic crises were taking place on the European continent, in both of which England was opposed to Germany. The first was the outcome of a rather trivial incident in September 1908 in which three German deserters from the French Foreign Legion were seized in a German legation in Casablanca. The second resulted from Austro-Hungarian annexation of the Balkan provinces of Bosnia and Herzegovina, which had been under the nominal sovereignty of Turkey, thereby precipitating a crisis with Russia and Serbia. Grey evaluated German behavior in the first episode in the light of an Anglo-German balance of forces that was becoming increasingly favorable to Germany; the crisis brought home to him the diplomatic implications of German shipbuilding, though it clearly did not convince some of his more skeptical Cabinet colleagues who forced the budget compromise. But it was the second crisis that led the government to satisfy the entire shipbuilding demands of the Admiralty. In March 1909 the confrontation in the Balkans was rendered most acute when Germany intervened on the side of Austria-Hungary, quickly compelling Russia to accept annexation of the Balkan provinces when Britain could offer no armed support to Russia in a Russo-German war. As these events were taking place, the British Admiralty came to conclude that its information about accelerated German building had been erroneous. Nevertheless, a strong Foreign Office argument was the decisive factor in the Cabinet's decision to build the contingent four dreadnoughts of the 1909 program. That argument was as follows:

(a) the Russian government (and therefore possibly also the French government) might be prone, in the aftermath of the Russian setback in the Balkans, to improve relations with Germany and Austria so as to avoid another similar humiliation;
(b) Great Britain might thereby find herself isolated from allies in relation to Germany; and
(c) British survival would depend on a larger naval superiority over Germany than had been realized previously.

(8) German shipbuilding was scheduled, according to the second navy law, to diminish from a total of four dreadnoughts in 1911 to two in 1912. The British Cabinet, which had reason enough to anticipate that the

projected slowdown would be realized in Germany, decided—in drafting the naval estimates for fiscal 1911—to bring about a reduction of £4 million in the British estimates by fiscal 1913. In July 1911, however, an Anglo-German crisis occurred when Germany sent a gunboat to the Moroccan port of Agadir to seek compensation for French actions in Morocco; and a speech later that month by David Lloyd George, the British Chancellor of the Exchequer, exacerbated the crisis even though it was intended to restrain the French.

Following this confrontation, the British Admiralty began to demand governmental approval of a new shipbuilding standard whereby England would have a sixty percent superiority over Germany in numbers of new dreadnoughts built. The new First Lord of the Admiralty, Winston Churchill, was sympathetic, having received intelligence from Germany to the effect that the latter's shipbuilding resources could enable it to overtake a narrow British margin of naval superiority. Moreover, Germany proposed altering the date on which her naval estimates were published, to follow rather than precede that of the British, in theory enabling her to gain rapidly on British strength in one year while following up that advantage in the next. The most serious aspect of the British strategic situation for Churchill, militating in favor of increased shipbuilding, was the German decision, announced in a January 1912 amendment to the navy law, to increase mobilized naval strength in home waters. The First Lord defended the sixty percent standard in the Cabinet and argued that a 2 : 1 ratio be maintained in response to all new dreadnoughts included in the navy law amendment (there were three in it originally). The Cabinet approved the new standards, choosing at first to build five new dreadnoughts in 1912, but reducing this number to four when Germany modified downward the shipbuilding terms of the navy law amendment.

There are also instances in which a period of severe tension was not followed by shipbuilding expansion. British naval expenditure in 1887, in the wake of acute Franco-German difficulties late in 1886, was lower than it had been the previous year, and not a single new battleship was begun. In the aftermath of the Anglo-French crisis at Fashoda in 1898, the British shipbuilding program for 1899 was designed primarily to push forward to completion vessels that had been sanctioned earlier. The British shipbuilding program of 1900, which followed a deterioration of Anglo-Russian relations provoked by Russian attempts during the Boer War to stir up a continental coalition against Great Britain, had the same general purpose. Similarly, the Dogger Bank crisis with Russia in October 1904, and the German challenge to the traditionally ascendant French position in Morocco in the spring of 1905 and again in the spring of 1906, had no appreciable effect on the shipbuilding competition. The British program of shipbuilding for 1905 consisted in the main of the famous *Dreadnought* and three battle cruisers, a numerical decrease from the previous year's program; and the British program for 1906 was actually revised downward after successful conclusion of the Algeciras conference of European powers called to settle the Moroccan problem.

Four plausible explanations account for the naval competition not adjusting to these crises, while being sensitive to others. They include (1) the element of technological change, already mentioned; (2) the unusual character of a crisis that made it somehow less serious from the British viewpoint, such as the confrontation provoked by Russian warships firing on British fishing vessels off the Dogger Bank in 1904 at a time when Russia was not only engaged in war with Japan but performing badly in it; (3) the failure of Britain's naval rivals to build up to levels anticipated by Great Britain—as in 1899 and 1900, when the extraordinary Russian program of 1898, on which the British Admiralty had gauged its own supplementary program of that year, was executed much more slowly than had been expected, and again from 1904 to 1906, when the failure of France and Russia to build up to British expectations brought about a downward modification of the British construction program in each of those three years after the program was first announced; and (4) the sometimes unusually compelling nature of budgetary limitations—as in fiscal 1905, when the British Cabinet in May 1904 prevailed upon the Admiralty on such grounds to reduce its naval budget for 1905.[7]

Giving due consideration to these exceptional cases, it is nevertheless conspicuous that the largest shipbuilding programs approved by the British government from 1884 to 1914 were affected by diplomatic crisis. These latter examples show that an armaments competition can be related significantly to changes in the perceived likelihood of war.

WEAPONS PROCUREMENT AND DETENTE

It is now necessary to discuss the impact on shipbuilding of a substantial reduction in the perceived likelihood of war, a condition of diplomatic détente. In a condition of détente between two or more nations, policymakers actively attempt to settle outstanding diplomatic or strategic issues of concern to them, and they are at least partially successful in doing so. Evidence in the period 1884-1914 suggests no significant relationship between procurement levels and the coming of détente; in general, apparently, the arms race does not slow down because of the coming of satisfactory diplomatic relations.

At least five instances appear in this period in which the pace of British shipbuilding, increased after a period of crisis, continued at a high level in a subsequent period of improved relations. First, improved relations between England and Russia in 1886 did not reverse the upsurge in British building begun the previous year. While no new vessels were started in 1886, British expenditure for new construction was only slightly less in that year than in 1885.

Second, improved relations between Britain and France and Russia beginning in 1894 did not reverse the thrust of the Spencer program, approved in England in March 1894. No large armored ships were begun in England in 1895; but even though Anglo-French détente persisted into the spring of 1896, the British undertook in that year the launching of a large new installment of naval construction to keep pace with French and especially Russian building.

Anglo-French détente beginning in 1902 (the so-called "era of good feeling") did not prevent the British from completing ships begun earlier, or from approving, in the autumn of 1902, and prosecuting a large shipbuilding program designed over a number of years to keep pace with French and Russian building. Again, a short interlude of improved Anglo-German relations in late 1906 and 1907 found both countries continuing to build dreadnought battleships, including additional installments.

Finally, Anglo-German détente returned during 1910-1911 and 1913, featured by resolution of disputes over economic concessions in Turkey and attempts to control the naval race between Britain and Germany. These diplomatic successes coincided with heavy additional construction installments as well as completion of ships already begun: five dreadnought battleships and battle cruisers were begun in England in each of the years 1910 and 1911, and five dreadnoughts in 1913.

The character of the strategic rivalry among states evidently has nothing to do with their propensity to cooperate diplomatically. Détente does not encourage the toning down of the competition but instead permits continuation of it, even though weapons accumulation is designed for a period of acute tension; hence the utility of stockpiling to the racers cannot be properly determined at a time of improved relations.

This unexpected feature of arms races complicates the effort to control them. For while improved diplomatic relations cannot be considered a sufficient requirement for controlling the competition (the delicate nature of the balance of forces and strategic requirements of the racers raise distinct questions of their own), they are at least a necessary condition. Yet even where nations do attempt to negotiate the difficult strategic issues associated with weapons races, as Great Britain and Germany did in the decade before World War I, détente, where present, did not exert a powerful salutary impact on the negotiations.

AN ARGUMENT FOR RELEVANCE

To this point, this paper has attempted to sort out regularities in the period 1884-1914, and has concluded that regularities associated with naval procurement do in fact exist in that time period. It will now be argued that, because arms races are recurring phenomena, regular and significant relationships highlighted in earlier periods should be reflected as well in other competitions at other times.

The failure of détente to bring a slowdown in a strategic weapons competition seems to be an uncomfortable feature of the present-day major superpower competition: the continuing American procurement of intercontinental ballistic missiles did not slow down with the improvement in Soviet-American relations after the Cuban missile crisis of 1962—an improvement particularly visible in such agreements as the Limited Test Ban Treaty of 1963. But to show the relevance of relationships revealed in the period 1884-1914, it is necessary to demonstrate that no more recent international development logically prevents earlier recurring patterns from recurring in the present as well. In particular, to defend the hypotheses derived earlier, some account must be taken of theories which maintain that world politics today is fundamentally different from that of earlier periods. At least five theories have been advanced to this effect:

(1) stable mutual deterrence among the superpowers has created a fear of war, reducing the perceived likelihood of hostilities irrespective of diplomatic endeavor;

(2) the bipolar distribution of power among the superpowers, in contrast to the multipolar distribution of earlier periods, significantly affects their propensity to go to war and also their arms race;

(3) the destructiveness of nuclear weapons does not permit their employment for any rational political purpose, hence the accumulation of nuclear weapons also serves no rational purpose;

(4) the Soviet-American competition is more qualitative than its predecessors, because of the rapidly changing nature of nuclear technology;

(5) in modern, technologically advanced societies, political pressures are posed by newly enfranchised groups of people for the

reallocation of governmental resources toward consumer and social concerns, and these pressures make it increasingly difficult for governments to sustain growing costs of defense procurement.

The first theory (Shulman, 1966)—which rests on the assumption that both superpowers are not only able to inflict retaliation that the opposing side would find unacceptable, in the event it contemplates aggression, but are content with this condition—overlooks the historic fact that the fear of war cannot alone assure that war will not occur. Great Britain became allied with Poland in 1939 to emphasize that Britain would not be indifferent to an attack on Poland by Germany, but Hitler nevertheless moved into Poland, triggering war with England. The Soviet Union introduced missiles into Cuba in 1962, despite statements by American leaders that such action would not be tolerated. Deterrence evidently can fail, and the risk of hostilities remains. But if this is so, then the likelihood of war can, in the context of deterrence policies, still become acute. The concepts of crisis and détente, which point up the wide variation in the likelihood of war among states that have not renounced hostilities, remain applicable in the nuclear age. They should have the same impact (or lack of it) on the Soviet-American competition as they had on competitions before World War I.

Some have argued that a particular distribution of power is more stable or less conducive to war than another.[8] But even if it is conceded that a world with six or seven great powers (as in the late nineteenth and early twentieth centuries) is more stable than a world of two great powers (as at the present time)—or the reverse—this does not mean that arms race processes are different in the two instances. Regardless of the number of active great powers, arms races are most easily waged by nations which place primary reliance on their own resources in providing for their security, even as they may be committed to the defense of other nations. The number of such so-called "security suppliers" need not be the same as, nor depend on, the number of great powers. Great Britain before World War I, like the United States after World War II, chose to wage armaments competitions irrespective of the attitudes of other powers, major or minor. Some nations find it necessary to rely on others for their security; such so-called "security consumers," as, for example, France before World War I and Communist China in the recent past, may attempt to behave as a security supplier by waging an arms race, but their ties to the policies of other powerful countries for assistance in case of war constitute a temptation to rely on the material help of those countries in peacetime as well.

The third theory, which assumes that the superpowers are unwilling to use nuclear weapons since by doing so they would destroy those values for which they are fighting (Morgenthau, 1964: 25, 35), misses the point that the caution of the superpowers in this regard does not mean their actual renunciation of the use of nuclear weapons. The United States is committed to defend the nations of Western Europe against Soviet attack and has acceded to the doctrine of the North Atlantic Treaty Organization, which contemplates first use of nuclear weapons in certain circumstances. The American intention to use nuclear weapons (even if it is not lived up to) is of fundamental importance to the United States, inasmuch as it is largely responsible for holding the NATO alliance together. The alternative strategy, of distinguishing between the rationality of nuclear and conventional weaponry in fighting wars, is vulnerable. The superpowers have nuclear weapons of small yield available that are of more potential usefulness than conventional explosives for tactical purposes, and the Soviet Union has always maintained that escalation would necessarily occur if a minor engagement were to be fought with the United States. Evidently nuclear weapons will continue to have a significant role in war and therefore also in peacetime weapons accumulation.

The fourth theory, that the Soviet-American competition is primarily technological, is supported by the rapidly changing nature of nuclear technology; nuclear weapons have become regarded as obsolete much more quickly than armaments which preceded them. Some have suggested (Aron, 1966: 428-429; Morgenstern, 1959: 19-20) that the current heightened technological rivalry is more conducive to war; another (Huntington, 1958: 55) believes it is less so. Both views may be in need of refinement, for this article must conclude that quantitative and qualitative rivalries in weaponry are themselves related. Perceived changes in the efficiency of strategic weaponry occasionally dampen the quantitative competition and occasionally accelerate it; the impact of the technological rivalry on weapons accumulation should not be neglected. Equally pertinent, however, are two additional observations. Apparently intense technological rivalry between the superpowers has been accompanied by quantitative competition as well, in the stockpiling of nuclear weapons and their means of delivery. Moreover, fears that strategic weapons would be subject to rapid obsolescence were rampant before the nuclear age. If the uncertainties of nuclear technology are thought of as unprecedented, then they should be evaluated as unprecedented in degree rather than kind.

The fifth hypothesis, focusing on constraints on the growth of military budgets from political demands on behalf of consumer interests and from insufficient resources,[9] must, if valid, be subjected to two caveats. First, in some conditions, the new political pressures may not bring a reallocation of resources from the defense to the consumer sector. In the United States after the second world war, new pressures for attention to social needs led to more government resources being allocated to the consumer sector, but resources allocated to the defense sector increased also. Evidently in some countries more resources can be made available for military *and* nonmilitary objectives than in others. Just when the growth in the national economy can no longer accommodate increasing governmental expenditure for both kinds of objectives cannot at this time be predicted. Further, attitudes that sustain worldwide commitments and growing defense arsenals can persist despite the rise of new pressures for attention to social needs, in part because of the efforts of vested interests to rationalize the traditional allocation of resources.

Second, pressures of an ongoing arms race may prevent a rethinking of resource allocation by actually bringing about a more permissive politics with respect to defense burdens. That is, an arms competition can lead vocal publics to accept larger defense burdens than they would have been willing to accept in the absence of the competition. It can also bring policymakers to alter prevailing notions of the amount of defense the national economy and the body politic can stand. For example, a Liberal British government could be formed in 1905 committed to reducing defense expenditures for doctrinal and political reasons, yet end up acquiescing in far greater defense expenditures.

Today, as previously, the great powers are highly prone to improve upon the quantity and quality of their weapons arsenals. If this article has been compelled to turn to previous instances of arms races, it is because—although sufficient information about the present-day nuclear competition is lacking—the problem of arms races remains of such compelling importance.

ON EXPLAINING
RECURRING ARMS RACE BEHAVIOR

Conditions that recur require explanation. Why does the coming of crisis often exercise an impact on the armaments competition, while the coming of détente does not? Some suggestive answers, still speculative but supported in varying degrees by the data of the historical cases examined in this study, will be advanced here. They must be refined with further study.

The first point to be made is that the coming of crisis in the period 1884-1914 demonstrated insufficiencies in the British capacity to make war. Sometimes a crisis, occurring in the midst of a deadlock among British governmental and naval leaders as to how the naval needs of the country should be defined, helped resolve the dispute in favor of the views of the navy:

(1) the occurrence of the Anglo-Russian confrontation in Central Asia in 1885 brought governmental approval, after a period of several months' indecision, of the famous two-power standard whereby Britain was to measure her naval needs in relation to two leading naval rivals, rather than only one. (The Admiralty's justification for the standard was that the prevailing British superiority over one naval rival would diminish to equality with that power, a condition tantamount to inferiority in relation to two powers combined.)

(2) The Anglo-American and Anglo-German confrontations of December 1895 and January 1896 helped resolve a budget dispute in the Cabinet provoked by the Admiralty's increased demands after a previous crisis.

On most occasions, however, the coming of a crisis emboldened naval officials to increase their demands, yet left the gaining of approval of these demands to the future:

(1) The creation and approval of the Naval Defense Act of 1889, whereby the British sought to have a fleet of battleships equal to the combined fleets of France and Italy by 1894, came about after the British government asked the Admiralty to draft a large shipbuilding program that would remedy British naval weakness in the Mediterranean.

(2) The Spencer program of 1894, in which provision was made to give the British battleship fleet a numerical equality with the combined fleets of France and Russia by 1898, was drafted in the hope that the persisting unfavorable British strategic position in the Mediterranean would not be exposed in the coming years; but that if it were, at least Britain would have enough strength to make war effectively against France alone.

(3) Approval of the supplementary program of 1898 came after the First Lord of the Admiralty interpreted a large Russian shipbuilding program as a potential challenge to the British capability to wage war against Russia in the Far East—a challenge whose importance was inflated in the light of the recent Port Arthur crisis, even as the British government was already committed to keep close pace with the course of Russian naval construction.

(4) Approval of the large shipbuilding program in the fall of 1902, which provided for a ten percent margin of British battleships over those of France and Russia by 1907, came after the First Lord spoke of his concern about possible German intervention in a war

pitting France and Russia against England—a threat dramatized in a recently acute Anglo-German dispute in the Far East.

(5) Approval of the large dreadnought program of 1909 and a one-power dreadnought standard aimed at Germany came after the Balkan crisis (pitting Austria and Germany against Russia) appeared to the British Foreign Office to have seriously weakened the common policies England, France, and Russia were previously thought to have had in relation to Germany.

(6) Approval by the Cabinet of the sixty percent dreadnought standard against Germany in 1912 came after another Moroccan crisis had underlined for the British government the importance of naval superiority over Germany, while at the same time triggering suspicions about German efforts to deny Britain that superiority.

The coming of crisis in some of these cases encouraged redefinition by the Cabinet of naval "supremacy" and approval of new enlarged force goals. This was true for the program approved in 1885, the Naval Defense Act, the Spencer program, the 1902 program, and the 1912 program. These examples show that Great Britain, traditionally respected by other nations as supreme on the seas, nevertheless chose to interpret "supremacy" in changing ways. The new interpretations became accepted as governmental policy during, or in the aftermath of, diplomatic confrontation, and with them came approval of enlarged force goals. But it is important to observe that the conception of the new force goals was often present before the onset of the crisis that led to its approval. Admiralty leaders in England created new force goals in response to shipbuilding actions taken by foreign powers and *not* in response to changes in the likelihood of war between Britain and those powers. Their constant preoccupation in shipbuilding matters was the pecking order of naval powers, and they frequently saw British naval supremacy in danger of being eroded. Why did these force goals not gain governmental acceptance earlier?

Clearly, in periods of diplomatic calm, intelligence was available to the British government which challenged the sufficiency of force goals: information indicated that foreign nations continued to augment their fleets, even in accelerated fashion; naval leaders occasionally claimed that foreign shipbuilding rendered the maintaining of previously agreed upon strategic requirements impossible. At such times this evidence was more irritating than convincing to those responsible for pursuing British diplomacy and for deciding upon the strategic requirements of the country. The information in the hands of British leaders of foreign shipbuilding and its bearing upon British strategic requirements was of a discrete kind, and they were able to rationalize it within their prevailing notions of British naval requirements. On the other hand, with the coming of a crisis and a challenge to British diplomacy from abroad, perceived hostile intentions were coupled with reports of foreign shipbuilding acceleration. British leaders were moved to alter force goals in such circumstances because, having received within a short period of time a great deal of alarming information about the intentions and capabilities of foreign nations, they were inclined to become alarmed about it.[10]

It is more difficult to explain why the arms race did not slow down with the coming of détente. From launching to the completion of a shipbuilding program or the fulfillment of a new force goal required a number of years,[11] during which the likelihood of war might have been, and occasionally was, significantly reduced. One explanation for the steady building pace in periods of improved relations, admittedly a partial one, is that shipbuilding activity was designed to impress other nations with British naval strength. Thus, in 1888 and 1894, British building programs were approved under pressure of Germany and Austria-Hungary as the price for these countries agreeing to continue to assist England against France and Russia in the Mediterranean. Attempts were also made to convince leading naval rivals of British strength. In 1896 the British government concluded that it could best discourage Russian naval expansion by keeping close pace with each new Russian shipbuilding proposal; a similar policy was adopted in 1912 in relation to Germany. These efforts bestowed importance on the process of constructing ships—and therefore militated against modifications in shipbuilding in times of détente—because they were designed as much to repair doubts about the credibility of British naval supremacy as about the reality of it.

A peculiar characteristic of an arms race is that it makes more difficult the satisfaction of minimum security requirements for the participants in the competition. Strategic balances and defenses are continually undermined in the course of the competition through development of more and better weapons systems. The point of this is not that it makes understandable the search for more exacting force ratios, but that it puts a premium on less material aspects of power. If the potency of military capabilities subject to competitive procurement becomes more uncertain, then, as Stanley Hoffmann (1967) argues, the importance of perceptions on the part of arms race participants can be expected to increase.[12] For the British government in the thirty-year period before World War I, the credibility of British naval supremacy in the eyes of both allies and rivals counted in strategic terms even more heavily than the actual ability to combat two leading naval rivals on favorable terms. British Foreign Ministers such as Lord Salisbury and Lord Rosebery, and later First Lord of the Admiralty Winston Churchill, used shipbuilding to strengthen respect for the British naval position by foreign powers.

The problem with this explanation of why the arms race did not adjust to improved relations is that it depends on a linkage between the diplomatic objectives of policymakers and the ongoing competition. The burden is to show that policymakers employed shipbuilding to facilitate diplomatic objectives. In many instances where large shipbuilding programs were launched, the published documents do not indicate that British policymakers employed shipbuilding for this purpose.

Of more general interest in explaining why the competition was not sensitive to détente is the character of the policymaking process, which has been highlighted in a number of stimulating writings (Schilling, 1962; Hilsman, 1971). In general, the process is a political one accentuating competition among the leading participants, but requiring some form of consensual agreement among them for policy to be determined. Sometimes agreement can be reached only with such difficulty that changing the policy becomes undesirable for the participants in the process, and the policy remains the same even when the external conditions which helped give rise to it have altered in the meantime. This "gyroscopic" effect of the policy process, as it has been referred to, is a consequence of the effort required to reach agreement among officials whose time is limited and whose concerns extend to policy problems that are substantively complex (Schilling, 1962: 26-27, 220-221). A consensus that was arrived at in a period of diplomatic strain and crisis can, because of the inertial nature of the policy process, endure in a period of détente.

Shipbuilding policy in Great Britain reflected the "gyroscopic" effect of the policymaking process insofar as the British government was all too seldom preoccupied in deciding what the policy underlying its shipbuilding effort should be. Major Cabinet debates on naval policy usually occurred at the start of shipbuilding programs (e.g., 1885, 1889, 1894, 1896, 1902, 1909, and 1912),[13] indicating not only that on many occasions a new consensus was required on policy before a program could be approved and launched, but also that consensus over policy was not something that could be easily disturbed. Policy, like shipbuilding, could go on and on. Once policy was decided upon and a program launched, there were no alternative policies spelled out for the Cabinet such that subsequent Admiralty requests in line with the program could be rejected or modified downward. The Admiralty was simply acting as the executor of the policy which the government had decided upon; only when the Admiralty itself criticized that policy as insufficient and suggested adoption of a new one did the Cabinet raise anew the question of what the naval policy of the country was to be.

Governmental consensus on naval policy took one of two forms. On some occasions, the government decided to build to a particular size of navy by a particular year, on the assumption that such dimensions were required to do battle with certain predetermined adversaries. The 1885 program, the Naval Defense Act (1889), the Spencer program, the 1902 program, and the 1909 program fall into this category;[14] they all were designed to enable the Royal Navy to combat other leading naval powers on favorable terms at some identified year in the future, despite the building plans of these powers. The second form of consensus found the government agreeing, not on the size of the navy ultimately required for doing battle with certain foreign powers, but on the need to keep close pace with the naval construction of other naval rivals who were perceived to be rapidly augmenting the size of *their* navies. This was sometimes referred to as a policy of "watching and waiting." In the cases of Russian building from 1896-1899 and German building from 1912-1914, the British government undertook to respond as quickly as possible to latest information of new projected building plans of Russia and Germany.

Of the two types of consensus, the more difficult to reverse, because it was so far-reaching, was the second. Once the government decided to respond with great sensitivity to all forms of shipbuilding in certain rival powers, it could not change this decision until it possessed credible evidence that the rival in question had slowed its shipbuilding rate. In the case of Russian procurement from 1896-1899, such strong evidence was provided by (1) official statements to British negotiators at the First Hague Conference of 1899, to the effect that the Russian government did not use British procurement as a standard for her own shipbuilding, but that her concerns were instead shipbuilding in Germany and Japan; and (2) indications that Russia was stretching out provisions of her large shipbuilding program of 1898. Having earlier overreacted to the Russian 1898 program with her own supplementary program of 1898, the British government could afford to and did relax somewhat its sensitivities about Russian shipbuilding. But it is not clear that evidence of shipbuilding slowdown in a naval rival was sufficient to alter the "watching and waiting" policy consensus. In the case of German procurement from 1912 to 1914, the German government's decision to delete a battleship from its 1912 amendment to the second German navy law brought an immediate deletion of two battleships scheduled for procurement on the British side (in line with Churchill's "naval holiday" proposal of 1912), but it did not alter the "watching and waiting" consensus. That consensus remained intact until the outbreak of World War I.[15]

All this leaves some provocative questions unanswered. How can a policymaking consensus, hinged upon weapons procurement by a strategic rival, be altered? Very little is known about how arms racers can reassure each other about their respective procurement intentions, provided they desire to do so.[16] Equally little is known about how accurately arms racers understand the policy processes in their respective adversaries. Certainly in the period 1884 to 1914, British leaders regularly interpreted the policies of their naval rivals as the consequence of monolithic goal seeking and goal determination; it would not be surprising that these rivals evaluated British policy in much the same way.[17]

The other type of consensus underlying procurement, that which was built around shaping a military arsenal to a particular size by a certain time, did not depend crucially, as did the first, on the behavior of a foreign power. It was sometimes subject to modification, however, in event of what was perceived to be especially threatening behavior by a naval rival. Thus, Russian shipbuilding late in 1895 led the government in England to reopen the issue of deciding what British naval policy, on behalf of which shipbuilding was pursued, should be. Yet there were instances where the British government fixed shipbuilding installments for future years in advance, in effect freezing the policy underlying shipbuilding. In the Naval Defense Act and 1902 programs, for example, the government decided upon programs in advance: in the first, for three consecutive years; in the second, for four. The advantage of this type of planning was that it insulated procurement from domestic political pressures, both inside and outside the government; the disadvantage was that it also insulated procurement policies from changes in world politics.

EPILOGUE

The thesis of Harold and Margaret Sprout (see note 9) raises some additional issues pertaining to the dynamics of arms races that might usefully be made explicit. These issues will be discussed here, in part to encourage further scholarly endeavor to understand the behavior of states in arms race conditions, and in part because the points of conflict between the Sprouts' thesis and the conclusions and assumptions of this paper create a new urgency to understand arms race behavior more fully and precisely.

Four factors seem to account for the differences between the Sprouts and myself. First of all, the Sprouts and I reason and argue from different sources of information. The evidence for the propositions advanced in this paper are derived from two cases of arms races, analyzed with the aid of a considerable amount of information. The Sprouts are impressed by changes that have developed over a much larger time span in (1) the amount of resources governments have required for undertaking political and military commitments in world politics, and (2) the ability of governments to underwrite the cost of these resources. Their investigation of the causes of the British retreat from empire (1968) is the major source of evidence supporting their reasoning on the matters that have interested them. That investigation led them to conclude (1968: 692) that "the British Empire became progressively insupportable as rising demands within Britain and resistance to imperial rule in the colonies coincided with escalating costs of maintaining Britain's historic role in international politics."

On the basis of their research on the British case, the Sprouts advanced the general hypothesis (1972: 293) that the international obligations of states have recently increased faster than their ability to pay for these obligations. They have suggestively stressed "the growing insufficiency of disposable resources" that "bedevils government at every level in America, and increasingly in other countries." But apart from usefully reminding us that the cost of international commitment, like the cost of everything else, has been going up recently, and reminding us further that new evaluations are in order to find out whether the gains achieved justify paying *all* the costs, the Sprouts do not explain why the costs of commitments should have risen to the point where they become generally more insupportable. Further, because they have not examined in detail how governments finance the cost of rising commitments, they have not furnished us with criteria to distinguish commitments that are supportable from those that are not.

A second difference between the Sprouts and myself has to do with the perspectives we employ to order the data available to us. My paper attempted to look at the perceptions British policymakers had about (1) the place of Britain in international politics; (2) the adequacy of British shipbuilding in the light of ongoing battleship programs of naval rivals; and (3) the character of the international political climate. It looked at these perceptions so as to reconstruct the process by which British decisions on battleship building were made. The paper is concerned in particular with documenting what bearing the perceived likelihood of war, which is subject to variation over time, has upon arms procurement in the short run.

The Sprouts have a perspective that is quite distinct from that adopted in this paper.[18] In their long and fruitful study of international politics, they have emphasized the factors of the environment, human and nonhuman, that define feasible behaviors for policymakers. The environment presents opportunities to policymakers insofar as resources are distributed so that they can be cheaply mobilized for desired policy undertakings; the environment presents limitations insofar as resources required for particular undertakings are unavailable or can be marshalled only very expensively. The Sprouts have stressed in their latest writings (1972: 306-307; 1971: 195) the limiting rather than the malleable character of the environment, because of the importance they attribute to a number of emerging trends, including (1) the growing propensity of those who perform essential services in advanced technological societies to become conscious of their potential leverage and to compete, stubbornly and often successfully, for scarce resources; (2) the growing despoilation of human habitats as an undesired by-product of technological endeavor; and (3) deepening social unrest fostered by urban decay and crime. The Sprouts (1972: 309) have linked these trends to a decline in the percentage of federal revenue in the United States allocated to military purposes; but they have said relatively little about the precise ways policymakers have perceived these trends, and more generally about the manner in which policymakers adjust their perceptions to keep pace with changing realities. On the other hand, they point out, most notably in their discussion of the British retreat from empire, that policymakers perceive selectively and sometimes mistakenly (Sprout and Sprout, 1971: 196-197), and that statesmen's images of their international role usually change slowly and lag behind events (1971: 369).

A third way in which the Sprouts and I disagree has to do with our expectations of change in attitudes and values of large populations. The period 1884-1914, from which evidence marshalled in this paper has been taken, shows remarkable constancy and stability in the attitudes of the British people toward national naval primacy. The vast majority of Englishmen supported naval expansion because they equated British security from external attack with a navy that was second to none. This attitude does not seem to have been contingent on the perceived likelihood of war between Britain and nations challenging British naval supremacy; rather, it depended on the perceived value of supremacy and the degree to which that supremacy was thought to be in danger. An important conclusion of the present paper, therefore, is that there is nothing about an arms race that diminishes popular support for a strong military posture and continuing adjustments to this end. Furthermore, the impact of an arms race in reinforcing attitudes favorable toward strategic procurement is evidently such that considerable counterpressures are necessary from other sources to reverse the supportive attitudes.

The Sprouts make some very plausible suggestions about the form and scale of the counterpressures necessary to reverse attitudes supportive of strategic procurement. Indeed, the Sprouts (1972: 309) write that the counterpressures already "appear to be working against the recent high level of support for the military establishment and military-related foreign policies" in the United States. They (1972: 309, 311, 313) identify three such counterpressures: (1) growing popular suspicions of governmental requests based on narrow nationalistic grounds; (2) attention to domestic needs during national security debates in the Congress; and (3) growing awareness of the staggering cost of American defense and international commitments. Though the Sprouts have not explicitly made allowance for the strategic nuclear arms race in this context, they presumably believe the impact of the still conspicuous Soviet-American competition on public attitudes will be ultimately overshadowed by the impact of factors they have listed.

Once again, it cannot be denied that the conditions to which they refer are becoming more salient in American politics, and in the politics of other advanced societies. Yet it is far from clear, notwithstanding these new factors, that Americans either widely expect the end of the Soviet-American competition or are widely complaining about the rising costs on the American side necessary to sustain it, as the recent debate over ratification of the Strategic Arms Limitation Agreements between the United States and Soviet Union will attest.[19] Efforts must be made to clarify what additional kinds of changes in the political climate, beyond those described by the Sprouts, must precede a major reversal of popular attitudes supportive of strategic procurement, and from where these changes will come. In particular, we need to learn which kinds of arguments for reducing defense budgets are persuasive to populations accustomed to hearing for so long that security is attainable only with considerable vigilance and at considerable cost.

A fourth and last difference between the Sprouts and myself is in the way we assess the meaning of technological change for state relationships. My paper found in its analysis of arms races continuing concern by policymakers about technological innovation by arms race competitors. In general, policymakers believed that the state of the art of battleship construction and changes in it affected the strengths of arms competitors, and they attributed special advantages to their more technically advanced competitors.[20] My study consequently attempted to trace these perceptions of policymakers and the ways in which they contributed to the behavior of states.

The Sprouts assess technological change in a very different way. They believe that the most recent consequences of technological change have raised fundamental questions about the quality of human life that cut across state boundaries (1971: 13-31). In their view, technical advances in military and non-military spheres have made states more *interdependent,* insofar as (1) the condition of life of any one national population is more closely a function of conditions of life elsewhere than ever before; and (2) what is done by policymakers in relation to problems of human life in one polity has growing reverberations for human life elsewhere. For this reason, technological change suggests to the Sprouts problems and opportunities common to all states; they believe that technological endeavor ties states together more importantly than it serves to divide them, insofar as states are all occupied increasingly with the health and survival of their peoples.

The strongest case for the validity of the Sprouts' assessment of technological change is that it allows them to highlight a set of values and priorities in human affairs that have been neglected. But the Sprouts' assessment may be plausibly advanced even in the light of the traditional priorities of policymakers and scholars—namely, national security, national power, and international responsibility. It has been suggested (Lambeth, 1972: 222-227; Basiuk, 1970: 36-37), for example, that the ability of arms competitors to translate technological innovation in weaponry design into strategic advantage declines as these competitors accumulate vast stockpiles of strategic weapons reliably deliverable to their targets. In particular, recent strategic procurement policies and deployments of the United States and the Soviet Union have rendered it more difficult for any aggressor to overwhelm the defender's capabilities without suffering a damaging blow in return. While an attacker could now conceivably make use of potentially more lethal forms of attack and of more efficient ways of reducing the effects of the defender's retaliation, the attacker's problem is magnified in the missile age by the fact that the defender's missiles and warheads have not only multiplied, but have been protected underground and beneath the oceans. Changes in the quantity and quality of the defender's forces have made more remote the possibility of new technology permitting any less-than-suicidal attack. Therefore, rivalry between the superpowers is less logically a function of technological change.

But the argument can be broadened further: if arms racers continue to maintain large capabilities to retaliate massively and devastatingly after suffering nuclear aggression, they will need indeed massive adjustments to change the balance of nuclear forces to a situation in which the benefits of attack become commensurate with the cost. In the difficulty any potential attacker faces in overcoming retaliatory capabilities of the defender is found additional security for both adversaries.

Even as technological developments in the design of weapons have less impact on the power and security of superpowers, technical advances in nonmilitary fields appear to be increasingly a source of social and political instability *within* them. For example, within the United States the technically sophisticated requirements of large organizations seem to have discouraged many potential recruits, whose aspirations have increased but who resist the specialization demanded by the organizations and direct their concerns instead to the solution of pressing social problems (Basiuk, 1970: 32-35). The confluence of these trends raises the possibility that future technological change could contribute more to the vulnerability of domestic governmental institutions than to the vulnerability of government to external attack—a condition which, if it can be documented, requires study. But this seeming paradox points to a wider and still more fundamental issue: whether the rising turbulence forecast by the Sprouts for the domestic politics of states in the future could be of such magnitude as to challenge the traditional security concerns of arms race competitors. There have been no efforts to explore what happens to an arms race when these traditional concerns, revolving around the balance of forces, are rivaled and overshadowed by others.

Most, if not all, scholarly writing on the subject of arms races has assumed, at least tacitly, that governments have the resources not only to procure strategic weapons according to some orderly criteria, but also to exercise domestic authority in such a way as to maintain social harmony and popular respect for governmental political institutions. The literature has also tended to assume that arms racers, preoccupied with many values, find the value of state security the most cherished, the most difficult to realize, and the costliest to seek. It seems appropriate now to question these assumptions, and to ask whether growing challenges to the authority of government from domestic sources could at some point bring about modifications of arms race behavior, insofar as major threats to governments are perceived by national leaders to come from within the body politic instead of from rival polities. That is, if we relax the assumption that the pursuit of security through an arms race automatically entails with it less complex and costly pursuit of other values, then we need to examine the consequences to the security pursuits of governments of the emergence of demands more difficult to satisfy than security from external attack.

To conceive of a state of world affairs in which the goal of security from external attack is more easily attainable than the goal of domestic tranquility is to invite more than speculation about current trends. It is to raise more generally the issue of what are the minimum (rather than the maximum) concerns of policymakers necessary to keep arms races alive; and conversely, what are the minimum prerequisites for bringing competitions to a close. Presumably, at some point a threshold would be reached where the largest and most compelling threats to authority and domestic tranquility are perceived by national leaders to come from within the body politic, and at that point policymakers would begin to disengage from an ongoing competition and perhaps cultivate solidarity of arms race adversaries to tackle complex domestic questions. Research is needed on the nature of this threshold and how it helps make state behavior less oriented toward interstate competition.

As the foregoing makes clear, to discuss different findings and the sources of these findings is to raise new issues for discussion. For the student of arms races, the most important of these issues raised in the present discussion are

(1) the supportability of more costly security commitments;
(2) the degree of sensitivity of political leaders to the limits of disposable resources in the wake of increasing demands on these resources;
(3) the impact, if any, of new public attitudes in support of consumer interests on older attitudes supportive of security spending;
(4) the relevance to the study of arms races of the multiple concerns of government;
(5) the relevance of changes in the concerns of government for the arms race behaviors of states; and
(6) the comparative impact of the domestic political process on governmental efforts to realize security and nonsecurity goals.

Different perspectives can contribute to our understanding of these issues, though there are also limits to the usefulness of different perspectives. For example, a study identifying the limits of feasible state behavior and the multiplicity of demands upon government can aid in identifying the consequences of particular decisions for the limited resources at the disposal of governments; but it cannot explain why governments sometimes exceed, in conducting particular foreign policy undertakings, the limits of what policymakers previously thought possible to sustain them. Such a study could identify the capabilities available to governments to pursue particular courses of action, but it could not explain why governments do not make the most efficient use of these capabilities. On the other hand, a detailed examination of the political process can reveal how conflict between policymakers leads to illogical and composite policy, and also how the political process helps strengthen efforts to facilitate one value and weakens efforts to achieve another. But it can illuminate only those behaviors that are the outcome of what policymakers perceive. That approach can duly note rising pressures for new governmental concerns, but it can cope with new "moral imperatives." only insofar as some powerful factions champion innovative approaches to the making of policy. The first study would inform us who pays for defense and in what proportion (e.g., Russett, 1970); the second would inform us *why* people do so. The first study would point to the inevitable diversity of human concerns; the second points best to what people feel strongest about, and what happens in the political process when different people feel strongly about totally different things.

These differences in focus strongly underline the need to make perspective explicit, and to be conscious of the limits of perspective in research pertaining to arms races, as in any other area of research. It is perhaps fortunate that scholars have different perspectives, because when they produce different findings from the data at their disposal, there is strong incentive for them to reinvestigate their perspective and reexamine the degree of precision that perspective brings to bear.

The paper to which this epilogue is attached attempted to explore the precise relationship between ongoing arms competition and variations in the perceived likelihood of war. Insofar as the paper identified this issue as a compelling one for scholarly understanding of arms races, it must argue also for those kinds of scholarly perspectives that most assist in the precise understanding of that issue. For the decision on a choice of perspective in any study depends not only on the degree of precision each affords in establishing assumptions and tools, but also on the degree of focus each supplies to the particular problem that is to be examined. The problem investigated in this paper—the manner in which governments adjusted to changes in the perceived likelihood of war—required a perspective that highlighted policymakers' perceptions of the international diplomatic climate and the balance of strategic forces. The problem also required a perspective sufficiently broad to connect the perceptions and perspectives of policymakers to governmental decision-making on strategic procurement. To be sure, choosing a particular perspective does not guarantee that it is sufficiently sharpened; efforts are needed, in understanding the politics of arms races (as well as other political phenomena), to inquire how the political process can be studied more effectively. But understanding the political process, difficult and cumbersome though this task may be, brings to bear much that is relevant to arms races which can be comprehended in no other way.

Different perspectives can suggest different answers and also different questions. But to understand the importance of perspective is no substitute for examination of the manifold problems posed by continuing, expensive arms competitions. Arms races are refractory problems for policymakers, as has been seen. But arms races are also refractory enough for scholarly observers in that the competitors seem to exhibit behaviors —understandable in political terms—that are if anything more inefficient, incongruous, and quixotic than political behavior usually is. To generalize about the phenomenon of arms races from the study of other political problems is perhaps to risk understating the paradoxical element of arms race activity. Even if this is so, it serves to make the politics of arms races a still more fascinating and worthwhile subject for study.

NOTES

1. The best statement on the recurring nature of arms races remains a monograph by Samuel P. Huntington (1958). The races analyzed in the present writing were chosen from a list of thirteen competitions, compiled by Huntington, taking place between the year 1840 and the present time. An incisive discussion of the current state of understanding of arms races is provided by Colin S. Grey (1971). Other surveys of the theoretical literature on arms races are included in the work of Martin C. McGuire (1965: 33-46) and Peter A. Busch (1970). McGuire and Busch provide summaries of the work of Lewis F. Richardson (1960), whose pioneering mathematical models of arms races emphasized the instinctual, mechanical aspect of policymakers' endeavor in arms race situations, and the dangers attendant in competitions where states compete on the basis of very shortsighted assumptions about their strategic needs and about the behavior patterns of their adversary. Kenneth Boulding (1962), Paul Smoker (1964), William Caspary (1967), and Jeffrey Milstein (1969) have endeavored to refine the work of Richardson.

The present study diverges in two ways from Richardson and those who have used his work as a foundation. First, it suggests that policymakers' reasoning and calculation are crucial in any effort to understand how policymakers adjust to an ongoing arms competition and what bearing arms races have to the security interests of states participating in them. Second, it suggests that the calculations of policymakers affecting the behavior of states in an arms race can change significantly over time, and therefore that a satisfactory understanding of the arms race behavior of states cannot be derived by assuming that policymakers' preferences on the subject of the competition are either inflexible or arbitrary. A recent outline of arms races, suggesting the major relevance of policymakers' calculations for the behavior of states in competitions, is provided by J. David Singer (1970).

2. To be sure, nations can and often do utilize instruments other than expansion of their warmaking capacities to enhance their security; they may try to attract allies or resort to force.

3. For pertinent bibliography concerning the two naval races to be discussed here, as well as detailed analysis of them, see an unpublished study by Barry H.

Steiner (1970). Professor John E. Moore assisted this study by allowing access to his rich collection of unpublished archival material pertaining to the British Admiralty.

4. A limitation of the present writing is that the information upon which its conclusions are based is largely published and therefore partial. However, more than adequate published information is available pertaining to the views of those leading British officials (such as the Prime Minister, Foreign Minister, and First Lord of the Admiralty) most intimately responsible for British foreign and naval policies. To see these policies through the eyes of these officials is to risk viewing them in one-sided fashion. But these officials were the most knowledgeable and influential on diplomatic and naval matters in the Cabinet. Therefore, the lack of full information about British Cabinet and Admiralty deliberations should not prevent recurring relationships in arms races from being reflected, if in fact such relationships exist.

5. Popular sentiment of pride in the British Empire and colonial endeavor contributed also to larger naval expenditure insofar as the connection was made between the importance of empire and the need for ships to sustain and protect it. I would distinguish here between (1) the permissiveness of popular mood that *allowed* increased expenditure, and (2) popular pressures that *helped to bring about* increased naval budgets. The permissiveness accruing from pride in Empire was joined, as the arms race evolved, with permissiveness from another source: resigned acceptance that the competition justified unprecedented defense burdens to keep pace with leading British naval adversaries (see, on this point, p. 21 of this paper). It becomes difficult to disentangle these two sources of permissiveness for larger naval budgets as the competition lengthened, but their combined effect was to prepare the British public to accept long term increases in the cost of strategic procurement without knowing or asking what the ultimate limit of the growth in these costs would be.

Vocal publics sometimes resorted to concerted pressure for increased expenditure on shipbuilding—notably in periods of "naval panic" highlighted by considerable emotional discussion that exaggerated the vulnerability of the British fleet in relation to the fleets of other powers. This pressure affected the bargaining within the British government in that it lent support to the shipbuilding demands of naval officials and sometimes (e.g., in 1884, 1893 and 1909, when naval panics had taken hold) led them to increase their demands. But the public impact on the size and the scope of British shipbuilding was not a major one; governments typically insisted on making decisions on the needs of the empire in an orderly fashion, and these needs were derived on the basis of information and criteria not known to the general public.

6. In this case, the Chancellor of the Exchequer exacted from the Cabinet, as the price for his concession, agreement that the estimates for the following year (fiscal 1897) would be reduced by an amount equivalent to the increase in 1896 above the previous year's shipbuilding expenditures (i.e., £600,000). But Russian naval construction, about which the British government was especially sensitive at this time, eventually led to reconsideration of the agreement and an active shipbuilding effort based on a policy of "watching and waiting" (see, on this policy, pp. 12-13, 26).

7. Often, however, budgetary constraints were not sufficient to hold back the pace of the competition. Agreement by a British Cabinet committee in February 1896 to reduce shipbuilding expenditure the following year did not prevent the reduction, as first announced, from being later whittled away to keep pace with Russian building. Similar agreement in 1911 came to nought in 1912 in the face of German building. Nor did the manner in which the coming of crisis was juxtaposed

with the drafting of the naval budget make any difference as to whether British naval construction adjusted to crisis. The British fiscal year began on April 1, with budget-drafting starting as early as the previous summer.

8. A statement of the controversy, along with a listing of the contenders on both sides, is provided by Michael Haas (1970: 98-99).

9. This argument has been made forcefully and provocatively by Harold and Margaret Sprout (1972; 1971). The Sprouts (1968) have given considerable attention to the British retreat from empire and extensive worldwide commitments, showing that this retrenchment is in large measure accounted for by the emergence of a new domestic politics in England. The response to the Sprouts in this and the following paragraphs is designed to show that serious reservations must be made when applying the lesson of the postwar British experience to the experience of great powers endowed with the capacity to prepare for and wage big wars. For a more extended appraisal of the divergences between the Sprouts and myself, the reader is referred to the epilogue to this paper.

10. This explanation was suggested by a hypothesis put forward by Robert Jervis (1968: 465-466). This explanation is more persuasive than an alternate one, namely, that British shipbuilding adjusted solely on the basis of British perceptions of the capabilities of leading naval rivals. To be sure, British estimates of adversary shipbuilding contributed to increases on the British side. In 1884, for example, Italian battleship building and Russian torpedo boat building led the British Admiralty to structure the projected program of shipbuilding for 1885 in the way it did; the burdens on the British navy for the future were clearly increased by shipbuilding in Italy and Russia at this time, as far as the Admiralty was concerned. In 1893, a large French shipbuilding program approved two years earlier was a major consideration, along with stepped-up Russian construction, in the British Admiralty's determination to press for a large battleship program in England. From 1895 to 1898, the Admiralty's main concern was the expansion of the Russian fleet, the danger from which was evident also to the Cabinet independent of Anglo-Russian crises in the period. In 1908-1909, Admiralty fears of an acceleration in German shipbuilding contributed to the content of the large program of naval construction proposed by the Admiralty in 1909. The point is that the coming of crisis did have a distinct impact on British shipbuilding because it added to the urgency attached by British policymakers to shipbuilding trends abroad. Factors other than the coming of diplomatic confrontation no doubt contributed to the perception of urgency; nevertheless, the role of diplomatic confrontation in this regard appears to be major.

11. The British usually consumed about three years to construct a first-class battleship; other major naval powers took up to three years longer.

12. As Hoffmann (1967: 58) aptly puts it: "When the physics of power declines, the psychology of power rises." He is referring to the current international system, but it seems clear that his remarks can apply to world politics in other periods of time.

13. There were two exceptions. One was the Cabinet debate early in 1901 triggered by Admiralty conclusions that construction of the Panama Canal and steady American battleship procurement would make the United States the second-ranking naval power within a decade; the Admiralty argued that England did not have the resources to keep pace with battleship construction in the United States along with that of leading European naval powers, and the Cabinet accepted this argument. The second exception was the debate of May 1904, when the Chancellor of the

Exchequer cited both popular clamor for greater nondefense spending and reduced construction by foreign powers to demand and gain Cabinet acceptance for reduced expenditure on the navy.

14. The case of the Spencer program was somewhat different here from the others, in that there was an agreement within the Admiralty to the effect that the program had a contingent element (see, on this point, p. 11). But there is no indication that the Cabinet either knew of, or was bound by, the terms of the Admiralty agreement.

15. The consensus was potentially threatened in 1914 by the Admiralty's growing attention to the shipbuilding policies of other foreign powers, particularly Russia. Churchill, for one, was anxious to control the Anglo-German competition even more tightly so as to leave the British freer to respond to the naval construction of less formidable powers, such as Russia, who were rapidly augmenting the size of their fleets.

16. Robert Jervis (1970), in a stimulating study about the ways states gauge and project each other's intentions, discusses weapons procurement only as an index of state behavior, not as a signal.

17. Graham Allison (1969: 695, 703) has suggested that some of the fears engendered in the Soviet-American strategic nuclear arms race can be explained by the propensity of American policymakers to view the Soviet government in distorted fashion as though it were a unified, cohesive body, intent on maximizing values, and closely examining the consequences of its actions.

18. In making this distinction between the Sprouts' perspective and mine, I am indebted to their work (1965) which first crystallized it and defended its importance in research bearing upon interstate relations.

19. The first stage of the Strategic Arms Limitation Talks (SALT) culminated in two agreements concluded in May 1972: one, a treaty limiting the United States and Soviet Union to the construction of no more than two antiballistic missile (ABM) sites and 200 ABM launchers; and the second, a five-year interim accord, in the form of an executive agreement, limiting the two countries in the construction of certain classes of offensive land-based and sea-based ballistic missiles. The effect of the interim accord was to freeze Soviet and American submarine-launched and land-based ballistic missiles at levels giving the Soviet Union superiority in numbers of launchers of these weapons systems, and it pointed toward further SALT negotiations encompassing *all* strategic offensive weapon systems (including strategic bombers and tactical aircraft). But the Senate debate on authorizing Presidential ratification of the interim accord showed considerable uneasiness over the quantitative ratios of Soviet and American ballistic missile launchers permitted under the accord, despite the administration's explanation that American technological superiority, particularly visible in multiple-warhead guidance systems already being installed on submarine-launched and land-based ballistic missiles, provided more than adequate security compensation. The uneasiness was reflected in Senate approval, and acceptance by the House of Representatives, of the following amendment sponsored by Senator Henry Jackson: "The Congress recognizes the principle of United States-Soviet Union equality reflected in the antiballistic missile treaty, and urges and requests the President to seek a future treaty that, inter alia, would not limit the United States to levels of intercontinental strategic forces inferior to the limits provided for the Soviet Union." This amendment reflects the hawkishness of the American political climate on defense matters despite the emergence of Soviet-American détente.

20. In the period 1884-1914, the British government most strikingly demonstrated its concern about technical innovation in the fleets of naval rivals when it evaluated the importance of the dreadnought battleship. England completed her first dreadnought in 1906, and by 1909 had come to discount her fleet of pre-dreadnought battleships so completely that it concluded British naval supremacy depended solely on dreadnoughts. See, for more details on this and other similar, if not so extreme instances, my earlier unpublished study (Steiner, 1970). For a general understanding of the importance attached by British naval leaders to technical achievements of naval rivals in this period, see Frederic Manning's (1923) biography of the long-time Director of British Naval Construction, Sir William White.

REFERENCES

ALLISON, G. (1969) "Conceptual models and the Cuban missile crisis." Amer. Pol. Sci. Rev. 63 (September): 689-718.
ARON, R. (1966) Peace and War (R. Howard and A. B. Fox, translators). Garden City, N.Y.: Doubleday.
BASIUK, V. (1970) "The impact of technology in the next decades." Orbis 14 (Spring): 17-42.
BOULDING, K. E. (1962) Conflict and Defense: A General Theory. New York: Harper & Row.
BUSCH, P. A. (1970) "Mathematical models of arms races," pp. 193-233 in B. M. Russett, What Price Vigilance. New Haven, Conn.: Yale Univ. Press.
CASPARY, W. R. (1967) "Richardson's model of arms races: description, critique, and an alternative model." International Studies Q. 11 (March): 63-90.
GREY, C. S. (1971) "The arms race phenomenon." World Politics 24 (October): 39-79.
HAAS, M. (1970) "International subsystems: stability and polarity." Amer. Pol. Sci. Rev. 64 (March): 98-123.
HILSMAN, R. (1971) The Politics of Policymaking in Defense and Foreign Affairs. New York: Harper & Row.
HOFFMANN, S. (1967) "Perceptions, reality, and the Franco-American conflict." J. of International Affairs 21, 1: 57-71.
HUNTINGTON, S. P. (1958) "Arms races: prerequisites and results," pp. 41-83 in C. J. Friedrich and S. E. Harris (eds.) Public Policy. Cambridge, Mass.: Harvard University Graduate School of Public Administration.
JERVIS, R. (1970) The Logic of Images in International Relations. Princeton: Princeton Univ. Press.
--- (1968) "Hypotheses on misperception." World Politics 20 (July): 454-479.
LAMBETH, B. S. (1972) "Deterrence in the MIRV era." World Politics 24 (January): 221-242.
McGUIRE, M. C. (1965) Secrecy and the Arms Race. Cambridge, Mass.: Harvard Univ. Press.
MANNING, F. (1923) The Life of Sir William White. London: John Murray.
MARDER, A. J. (1940) The Anatomy of British Sea Power. New York: Alfred A. Knopf.
MILSTEIN, J. S. and W. C. MITCHELL (1969) "Computer simulation of

international processes: the Vietnam war and the pre-World War I naval race." Peace Research Society Papers 12: 117-136.
MORGENSTERN, O. (1959) The Question of National Defense. New York: Random House.
MORGENTHAU, H. J. (1964) "The four paradoxes of nuclear strategy." Amer. Pol. Sci. Rev. 58 (March): 23-35.
RICHARDSON, L. F. (1960) Arms and Insecurity: A Mathematical Study of the Causes and Origins of War. Pittsburgh: Boxwood.
RUSSETT, B. M. (1970) What Price Vigilance. New Haven, Conn.: Yale Univ. Press.
SCHILLING, W. R. (1962) "The politics of national defense: fiscal 1950," pp. 1-266 in W. R. Schilling et al., Strategy, Politics and Defense Budgets. New York: Columbia Univ. Press.
SHULMAN, M. (1966) Beyond the Cold War. New Haven, Conn.: Yale Univ. Press.
SINGER, J. D. (1970) "The outcome of arms races: a policy problem and a research approach." Presented at the Third General Conference of the International Peace Research Association.
SMOKER, P. (1964) "Fear in the arms race: a mathematical study." J. of Peace Research 1: 55-63.
SPROUT, H. and M. SPROUT (1972) "National priorities: demands, resources, dilemmas." World Politics 24 (January): 293-317.
--- (1971) Toward a Politics of the Planet Earth. New York: Van Nostrand Reinhold.
--- (1968) "The dilemma of rising demands and insufficient resources." World Politics 20 (July): 660-693.
--- (1965) The Ecological Perspective on Human Affairs, with Special Reference to International Politics. Princeton: Princeton Univ. Press.
STEINER, B. H. (1970) "Arms race processes and hazards." Ph.D. dissertation. Columbia University.
WIESNER, J. (1967) "The cold war is over but the arms race rumbles on." Bull. of Atomic Scientists 13 (June): 6-9.
--- (1966) "Disarmament and European security," pp. 463-468 in United States Policy Toward Europe (and Related Matters), Hearings before the Committee on Foreign Relations, U.S. Senate, Eighty-Ninth Congress, Second Session. Washington, D.C.

BARRY H. STEINER was born in Los Angeles in 1942. He received his undergraduate degree from the University of Southern California, followed by graduate study at Georgetown University. His advanced graduate work was taken at Columbia University, where he was awarded the doctoral degree. While serving as a member of the faculty at California State University, Long Beach, he is currently preparing a study of the theories held by national leaders about the dynamics of arms races.